CLASSIC ROCK FOR TWO

T0079054

Arrangements by Peter Deneff

ISBN 978-1-5400-6541-4

HAL•LEONARD®

Visit Hal Leonard Online at
www.halleonard.com

Contact Us:
Hal Leonard
7777 West Bluemound Road
Milwaukee, WI 53213
Email: info@halleonard.com

In Europe contact:
Hal Leonard Europe Limited
42 Wigmore Street
Marylebone, London, W1U 2RN
Email: info@halleonardeurope.com

In Australia contact:
Hal Leonard Australia Pty. Ltd.
4 Lentara Court
Cheltenham, Victoria, 3192 Australia
Email: info@halleonard.com.au

BANG A GONG
(Get It On)

CLARINETS

Words and Music by
MARC BOLAN

CAN'T FIGHT THIS FEELING

CLARINETS

Words and Music by
KEVIN CRONIN

Rock Ballad

CARRY ON WAYWARD SON

CLARINETS

Words and Music by
KERRY LIVGREN

Moderate Rock

COLD AS ICE

CLARINETS

Words and Music by MICK JONES
and LOU GRAMM

COME ON EILEEN

CLARINETS

Words and Music by KEVIN ROWLAND,
JAMES PATTERSON and KEVIN ADAMS

COME TOGETHER

CLARINETS

Words and Music by JOHN LENNON
and PAUL McCARTNEY

CROCODILE ROCK

CLARINETS

Words and Music by ELTON JOHN
and BERNIE TAUPIN

DOWN ON THE CORNER

CLARINETS

Words and Music by
JOHN FOGERTY

EVERY LITTLE THING SHE DOES IS MAGIC

CLARINETS

Words and Music by
STING

Moderately fast

FREE FALLIN'

CLARINETS

Words and Music by TOM PETTY
and JEFF LYNNE

HURTS SO GOOD

CLARINETS

Words and Music by JOHN MELLENCAMP
and GEORGE GREEN

THE JOKER

CLARINETS

Words and Music by STEVE MILLER,
EDDIE CURTIS and AHMET ERTEGUN

LIVIN' ON A PRAYER

CLARINETS

Words and Music by JON BON JOVI,
DESMOND CHILD and RICHIE SAMBORA

MAGGIE MAY

CLARINETS

Words and Music by ROD STEWART
and MARTIN QUITTENTON

MR. ROBOTO

CLARINETS

Words and Music by
DENNIS DeYOUNG

MONEY FOR NOTHING

CLARINETS

Words and Music by MARK KNOPFLER
and STING

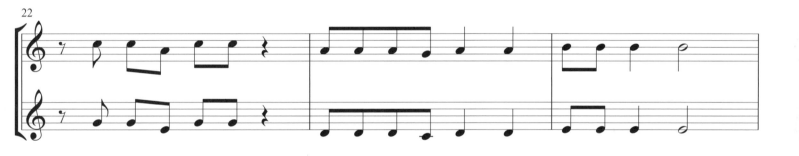

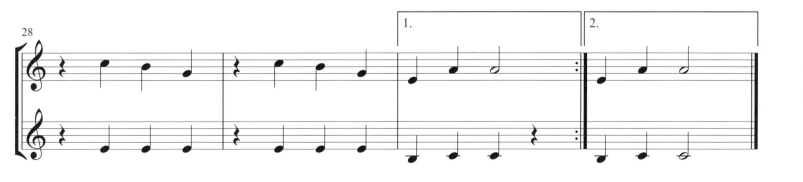

ONE MORE NIGHT

CLARINETS

Words and Music by
PHIL COLLINS

PEACE OF MIND

CLARINETS

Words and Music by
TOM SCHOLZ

Medium fast

REELING IN THE YEARS

CLARINETS

Words and Music by WALTER BECKER
and DONALD FAGEN

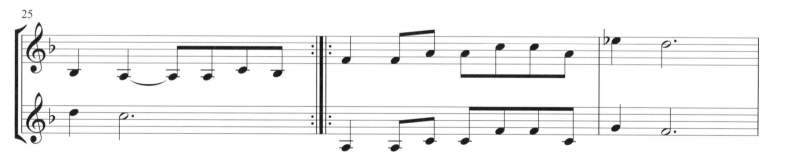

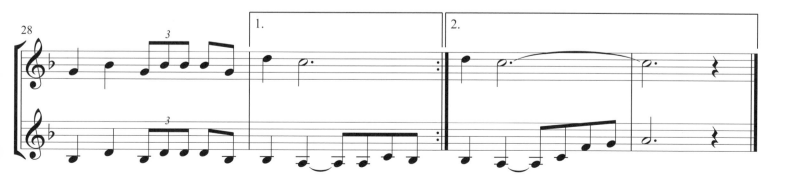

SMOKE ON THE WATER

CLARINETS

Words and Music by RITCHIE BLACKMORE,
IAN GILLAN, ROGER GLOVER,
JON LORD and IAN PAICE

SUMMER OF '69

CLARINETS

Words and Music by BRYAN ADAMS
and JIM VALLANCE

UPTOWN GIRL

CLARINETS

Words and Music by
BILLY JOEL

YOU'RE THE INSPIRATION

CLARINETS

Words and Music by PETER CETERA
and DAVID FOSTER

Rock Ballad